The Promise: The Amazing Story of Our Long-Awaited Savior
Copyright © 2021 by Jason Helopoulos
Illustrations © 2021 by Crossway
Published by Crossway
1300 Crescent Street
Wheaton, Illinois 60187

Published in association with the literary agency of Wolgemuth & Associates.
Cover design: Rommel Ruiz
First printing 2021
Printed in China
Hardcover ISBN: 978-1-4335-7106-0
Library of Congress Cataloging-in-Publication Data

    Names: Helopoulos, Jason, author. | Ruiz, Rommel, illustrator.
    Title: The Promise : The Amazing Story of Our Long-Awaited Savior / Jason
      Helopoulos; illustrated by Rommel Ruiz.
    Description: Wheaton, Illinois : Crossway, 2020. | Audience: Ages 8–12 |
      Audience: Grades 2–6
    Identifiers: LCCN 2020031839 | ISBN 9781433571060 (hardcover)
    Subjects: LCSH: Jesus Christ—Messiahship—Biblical teaching—Juvenile
      literature.
    Classification: LCC BT230 .H12 2020 | DDC 232/.12—dc23
    LC record available at https://lccn.loc.gov/2020031839

Crossway is a publishing ministry of Good News Publishers.

RRDS		31	30	29	28	27	26	25	24	23	22	21
15	14	13	12	11	10	9	8	7	6	5	4	3	2	1

THE
PROMISE

THE AMAZING STORY OF
OUR LONG-AWAITED SAVIOR

WRITTEN BY

JASON HELOPOULOS

ILLUSTRATED BY

ROMMEL RUIZ

CROSSWAY • WHEATON, ILLINOIS

———————————

"Christ is the sum of the whole Bible, prophesied, typified, prefigured, exhibited, demonstrated, to be found in every leaf, almost every line, the Scriptures being but as it were the swaddling bands of the child Jesus."

THOMAS ADAMS

"Think of Christ as the very substance, marrow, soul, and scope of the whole Scriptures."

ISAAC AMBROSE

In the beginning, God was there.
And God created the heavens and the earth.

On the very first day
God separated the light from the darkness.
The light he called Day,
and the darkness he called Night.

On the second day
God created the heavens in the midst of the waters,
and God separated the heavens from the waters.

On the third day
God gathered the seas together,
and he made the dry land appear.
And God made all the plants and trees and vegetation,
and God saw that it was good.

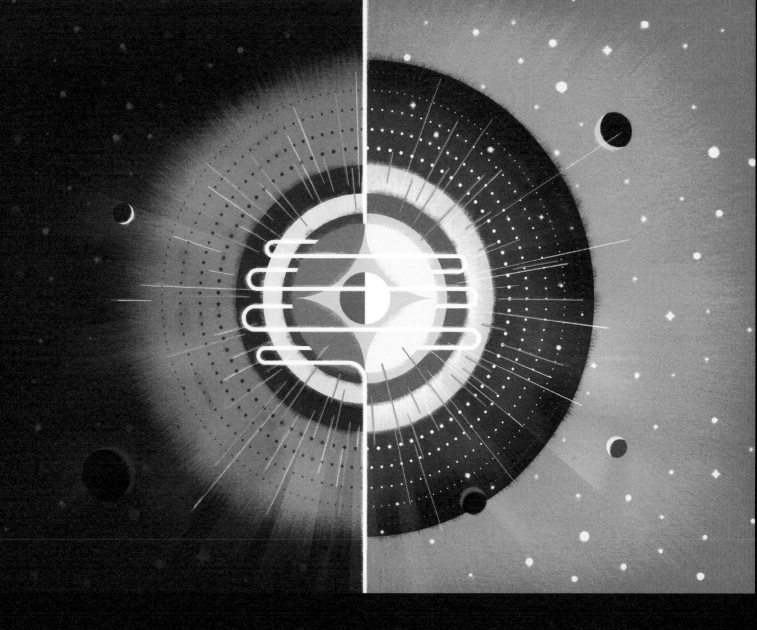

On the fourth day
God made the sun and the moon and the stars—
the sun and the moon to rule over the Day and the Night.
And God saw that it was good.

On the fifth day
God made all the birds, filling the sky.
And God filled the seas with fish and great sea creatures.
And God blessed them.

On the sixth day
God made the earth bring forth every kind of living creature,
livestock and creeping things and all the beasts of the earth.

Then God created man and woman in his own image—
more prized than the tall trees,
the beautiful flowers, the powerful beasts,
even the great sea creatures and stars in the sky—
for God created man and woman alone in his image.

This man and woman enjoyed the earth with God.

In fact, they were friends with God.
They walked with him in the cool of the day.

And God saw everything he made.
He saw that everything was good—in fact,
it was very good.

Until it wasn't!

The worst of all days came—
a day angels could not have imagined,
a day mankind has forever regretted,
a day only God could save us from.

That day a serpent came with a lying tongue, and the first man, Adam, and the first woman, Eve, listened to this lying serpent.

They listened to his lies and believed him instead of God.
And they sinned against God—losing everything.

Mankind lost holiness.

Mankind lost righteousness.

Mankind lost life.

But worst of all, no longer could people be with God.

No longer was God their friend,

because they chose not to trust God.

But God gave mankind a promise.
And what a great promise it was!
The promise of salvation!
He promised that one would come who
would crush the head of the lying serpent,
one who would deliver mankind from their sin,
one who would restore man and woman's
relationship with God.

Who will this one be?

Maybe a really good man can save us,
a really good man like Noah,
whom God saved from the flood so that he and his family
could once again fill the earth with people.

But Noah emerged from the ark
and almost immediately sinned against God.
We see that not even a really good man
like Noah can save us.

Maybe a great man of faith can save us,
a great man of faith like Abraham,
the father of the nation of Israel.

But Abraham feared other men and lied about Sarah,

calling her his sister and not his wife.

We see that not even a faith-filled man like Abraham can save us

Maybe a great prophet can save us, a great prophet like Moses, who led the people of Israel out of slavery in Egypt.

But Moses lacked faith, striking the rock twice, and disobeyed God.
We see that not even a great prophet like Moses can save us.

Maybe a great conqueror can save us,
a great conqueror like Joshua, who led the people into the land.

But Joshua didn't conquer as he was told, and left rebellious people in the land.
We see that not even a great conqueror like Joshua can save us.

Maybe a great judge can save us,
a great judge like Samson, who delivered the people from their enemies.

But Samson gave his heart to a woman over God.
We see that not even a great judge like Samson can save us

Maybe a great king can save us, a king like Saul,
who was stronger and taller than all the other men.

But Saul was gripped by pride. He did not seek God's glory, only his own.

We see that not even a great king like Saul can save us.

Maybe a man after God's own heart can save us,
a man like David, who loved and worshiped God.

But David sinned a great sin with a woman named Bathsheba.
We see that not even a man after God's own heart like David can save us.

Maybe a great priest can save us,
a priest like Eli, who could speak to God for mankind.

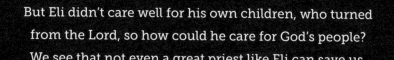

But Eli didn't care well for his own children, who turned
from the Lord, so how could he care for God's people?
We see that not even a great priest like Eli can save us.

If no mere man or woman can save us,
then maybe trusting in other things can.

Some tried to obey the law of God—all his Ten Commandments and even more.
But they could not keep his law perfectly.
Not even trying to obey the law of God perfectly can save us.

Maybe the sacrifices required by the law could save them from their sins.

But even though they brought animals to sacrifice, it never seemed to truly cover their sin.

All seemed lost.

Who or what can save us?

Four hundred years of silence,
and then God broke the silence.
A child was born, Immanuel, God with us.
He was given the name Jesus,
because he would save his people from their sins.

In this child, the promise came.
He was the one who would crush the head of the serpent,
deliver mankind from their sin, grant them his righteousness,
work in them his holiness, give them his life.

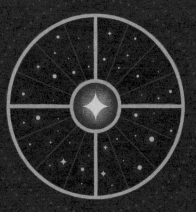

But best of all . . . he secured his people's relationship with God.
Once again, people could be with God. Forever, God would be their friend.
There has never been and never shall be a Savior like this.

He is unlike any other man
or woman who came before.

Jesus is the perfect
righteous man.

Jesus is the perfect
faith-filled man.

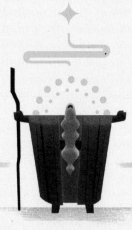

Jesus is the perfect
Prophet of God.

Jesus is the
perfect conqueror.

Jesus is the
perfect Judge.

Jesus is the
perfect King.

Jesus is the perfect man
after God's own heart.

Jesus is the
perfect law keeper.

Jesus is the
perfect great priest.

Jesus is the
perfect sacrifice.

Jesus is the perfect
offering to God.

Jesus was and is the promised one,
the perfect one,
the one who would not and could not sin,
the one great Savior of men and women.

Do you know this promised one?

Have you trusted in him so that you are friends with God?

KEY BIBLE PASSAGES FOR FAMILY READING

The Creation of the World: Genesis 1–2

The Fall of Man: Genesis 3

The Life of Noah: Genesis 6–9

The Life of Abraham: Genesis 11–25

The Life of Moses: Exodus; Numbers

The Life of Joshua: Joshua

The Life of Samson: Judges 13–16

The Life of Saul: 1 Samuel 9–31

The Life of David: 1 Samuel 16–31; 2 Samuel; 1 Kings 1–2

The Life of Eli: 1 Samuel 1–4

The Ten Commandments: Exodus 20; Deuteronomy 5

The Sacrificial Law: Leviticus 1–17

The Coming of Jesus: Matthew 1–2; Luke 2; John 1

The Death and Resurrection of Jesus:
   Matthew 27–28; Mark 15–16; Luke 23–24; John 19–20

Jesus Fulfills the Old Testament:
   Romans 5; Galatians 3–4; Colossians 1; Hebrews 1–10